WRITING ON
OUR HEARTS

WILD SIDE PUBLISHING
Auckland, New Zealand
www.wildsidepublishing.com

ISBN Softcover 978-1-991299-57-4
ISBN EPub 978-1-991299-58-1

Words added in parentheses in Scripture references are the author's own.

Unless otherwise noted, all Scripture is taken from the New King James Version. Copyright © 1982 by Thomas Nelson, Inc. Used by permission. All rights reserved.

Scripture quotations marked NLT are taken from the Holy Bible, New Living Translation, copyright © 1996, 2004, 2015 by Tyndale House Foundation. Used by permission of Tyndale House Publishers, Inc., Carol Stream, Illinois 60188. All rights reserved.

Scripture quotations marked ESV are from The Holy Bible, English Standard Version®, copyright © 2001 by Crossway, a publishing ministry of Good News Publishers. Used by permission. All rights reserved.

Scripture quotations marked MSG are taken from THE MESSAGE, copyright © 1993, 2002, 2018 by Eugene H. Peterson. Used by permission of NavPress. All rights reserved. Represented by Tyndale House Publishers, a Division of Tyndale House Ministries.

Scripture quotations marked NIV are taken from the New International Version®, NIV®. Copyright © 1973, 1978, 1984, 2011 by Biblica, Inc.™ Used by permission of Zondervan. All rights reserved worldwide.

Cover photo by Art Lasovsky (www.unsplash.com). Used with Permission.

Typeset in Poppins and Minion

Cataloguing in Publishing Data
  Title: Writing on our Hearts
  Author: Peter Emmanuel
  Subjects: Christian life and ministry; discipleship; faith and life; biblical
    studies; pastoral resources.

A copy of this title is held at the National Library of New Zealand.

Writing on our Hearts

Living as Expressions of God's Love

PETER EMMANUEL

"In the time I have served alongside Peter in local church ministry, I have known him to be a man after God's heart. A man of integrity, dedication, wisdom, and grace. A man unafraid of stepping outside of his comfort zone to serve God in challenging places. I pray that this book will be a blessing to all who read it, as it has been to me."

— Rev. Matt Chapman
Minister, Howick Presbyterian Church, Howick

"This book is a beautiful testimony that unpacks the foundations of the Christian life—from the amazing grace of God to the power of community. The words on these pages communicate the Gospel in a way that will draw you into the story of God and his redemptive plan for humanity."

— Pastor Steve Green
Senior Pastor, Elim Christian Centre, Auckland

"What an amazing book—true to Scripture, spiritually uplifting, and very personal! I know Peter as a man with a deep and real love for the Lord and for people. He is someone who 'walks the talk'. I admire his commitment to the Lord in spite of adversities. Please read this book! The way Peter presents and discusses Scripture releases its power, making this book a must-read for anyone seeking to be emboldened in their faith."

— Rev. Johan Hendriks
Minister, Afrikaanse Christen Kerk of New Zealand

Dedicated to everyone facing challenging times and searching for answers to life's big questions.

In memory of our dear parents Hepzibah & G Emmanuel and Mary Jane & D Henry Paul, who were responsible for nurturing my faith in our Lord Jesus Christ.

FOREWORD

I am honoured to be invited by Brother Peter to write the foreword to his book, *Writing on Our Hearts*. This writing is undoubtedly Spirit-led and is a wonderful source of practical wisdom and guidance which may be applied to various areas of our lives. The topics in this book are substantiated by Scripture. May you be encouraged as you read about:

- how Peter's godly upbringing has kept him in good stead to follow and serve the Lord diligently along with his wife Harshala. This will challenge us to live in a godly way (Proverbs 22:6).
- the importance of declaring God's word (2 Corinthians 4:13).
- the compassion of the Lord which has been extended to us so that we can be a blessing to others (Galatians 5:22-23 & Proverbs 11:25).
- the necessity to fulfil the Great Commission (Daniel 12:3).
- the beauty of God's grace (2 Corinthians 12:9 & Romans 3:23-24).
- the importance of interdependence (Hebrews 3:13 & 10:24-25).
- how, as long as we live, we will have tribulation (Acts 14:22).
- how in everything, we must give thanks to the Lord (1 Thessalonians 5:18).

- how we must live a pure, holy, and victorious life and eagerly prepare for the Lord's return (Hebrews 12:14).

May this foreword serve as an entrée in anticipation of enjoying the main meal! The Lord bless you!

Ps. Robin John
Eternal Life Ministries, Perth, Australia

CONTENTS

AUTHOR'S NOTE

"But let him who glories glory in this, that he understands and knows Me, that I am the Lord, exercising lovingkindness, judgment, and righteousness in the earth. For in these I delight," says the Lord.
Jeremiah 9:24

To truly love and follow the Lord is to recognise Him as our Saviour and guide.

God delights in kindness, justice and righteousness, and His words always come to pass, whether quickly or over time. We see this in Daniel's interpretation of God's message to King Belshazzar. Likewise, the promise of Genesis 3:15 was fulfilled through Jesus Christ thousands of years after it was given. Despite humanity's sin, God patiently awaited the right time to send our Saviour.

When I was only eight, my father passed away, leaving our family in financial and emotional hardship. Growing up fatherless was incredibly hard. I struggled with fear, loneliness and anxiety, but praying with my dear mother and siblings was a source of comfort. In 2009, God assured me that all prayers are answered with a 'yes', 'no', or 'wait'. My testimony is that His plans are always the best. We also know that God calls us to obedience.

As we navigate life's challenges, our actions should glorify Him. May these reflections encourage you in every season. God bless you!

Moses Peter Rajkumar Emmanuel
Jesu Beracah Ministries
New Zealand, May 2025

1
—

THE LETTER OF
OUR LIVES

In the Oxford English Dictionary, the meaning given for the word *epistle* is 'letter'. A letter tells a story; it is made interesting when it includes challenges faced by the writer and captures how he or she handled or overcame the challenge. At the end of the letter, we often hear of the accomplishments of the writer. Reading between the lines, one can make out the attitude of the writer, what motivated him or her, and how determined or focused the writer was in pursuing what he or she wanted to narrate.

It is the same with the Christian's walk in this world. In his letter to the Corinthians, the apostle Paul tells the members of the church in Corinth that they are like epistles (or *letters*) written on the hearts of their leaders or mentors. He goes on to state that these believers are *epistles of Christ,* written by the Spirit of the living God on 'tablets of flesh', that is, on the heart.

> *"You are our epistle written in our hearts, known and read by all men."*
>
> 2 Corinthians 3:2

What 'letter' are people reading when they look at our life with all its challenges, distractions, and responsibilities? We must remember that we are an epistle to the world around us, through which the nature and character of God are known and read by men. When the life-giving Spirit of God writes upon our hearts, our lives become a letter that brings life into those we interact with. Our job, then, is to pursue His purposes in our lives with determination and care. It may take many manoeuvres and careful steering to stay on the course God has for us, but we can do this with the help of the Holy Spirit. In fact, living a Holy Spirit-led life is the only way to become an effective *epistle of God* in this world full of misplaced priorities and self-centredness.

The Scriptures are full of examples of those whose lives testified to the grace and power of God. The foremost example is our Lord and Saviour Jesus Christ. Standing up in the synagogue, he quoted from the book of Isaiah:

> *"The Spirit of the Lord is upon Me, because He has anointed Me to preach the gospel to the poor; He has sent Me to heal the brokenhearted, to proclaim liberty to the captives and recovery of sight to the blind, to set at liberty those who are oppressed."*
>
> *Luke 4:18*

Whenever Jesus Christ was moved with compassion for the people, the sick were healed. He even fed the hungry when they were away from home and had a long way to go back. As ambassadors for Christ, we also need to show love to people all around us and thereby lead them to Christ. Others should know that we are Christ's disciples because we demonstrate love for one another (John 13:35). We are to be filled with the compassion of Christ, empowered with the knowledge that we belong to Him, and guided and directed by God's wisdom to carry out what He wants us to do.

When we are led by God's Spirit, we carry the authority in the name of Jesus Christ to bring healing and set free those who are oppressed and in bondage. We bring sight to the blind— blindness that is still holding many from knowing the Lord Jesus Christ. *Where the Spirit of the Lord is, there is liberty.*

The early church understood this 'ministry of the Spirit'. The apostle Paul addresses the Thessalonians by saying that God saved them, not only through the message of salvation, but also with *the power of the Holy Spirit,* revealing the full assurance that what was said was true. The Thessalonians received the message with joy in spite of the severe suffering this brought them. Paul commends them, saying that they had imitated not only him and his team, but the Lord. As a result, they became an example to all the Christians in Greece. 1 Thessalonians 1:8 tells us that "the word of the Lord rang out from them to people everywhere, even beyond Greece."

The Spirit of Encouragement

Jesus calls us to be salt and light, to 'add flavour' and be an encouragement to people around us (Matthew 15:13-16). When we are on the mountaintop of life, we need to be sensitive to those in need around us. When we are at the low points of our lives, we should not wallow in self-pity, nor should we allow sorrow or grief to drown us. We need to search for opportunities to bless others wherever we can and be an encouragement to them.

Are you facing a Goliath-like situation in your life? Are you faced with the reality that you do not have the height, strength or skillset to fight and overcome the situation? Do you have the faith to carry the pebbles and the sling in the name of Almighty God to fight the enemy and be victorious? We must remember that the weapons of our warfare are not carnal, but they are mighty. We need to keep praising God for all that He has been doing in our lives and what He is going to accomplish.

The Spirit of Wisdom

Relying on our own strength and intellect can take us to a certain level of achievement in terms of our goals. We will, however, meet challenges and be required to make decisions that are outside our understanding and knowledge. Even with great determination and the mindset of a go-getter, we are often left with the problem at hand unresolved. Like Shadrach, Meshach and Abednego, when we are faced with a dilemma, we must choose to turn to our Creator, the fountain of all wisdom. Listen to their response to the King of Babylon:

> *"King Nebuchadnezzar, we do not need to defend ourselves before you in this matter. If we are thrown into the blazing furnace, the God we serve is able to deliver us from it, and He will deliver us from Your Majesty's hand. But even if He does not, we want you to know, Your Majesty that we will not serve your gods or worship the image of gold you have set up."*
>
> *Daniel 3:16-18*

The three men in the furnace started with the right perspective; they depended on God right from the beginning. Like them, the choice is ours. We have the freedom to rely on our own wisdom, or to choose the path that will bring God the most glory. When we allow the Holy Spirit to lead us through any situation, we will be able to rest assured that our steps have been directed by Him in our journey of faith. Philippians 4:6-7 encourages us:

"Be anxious for nothing, but in everything by prayer and supplication, with thanksgiving, let your requests be made known to God; and the peace of God, which surpasses all understanding, will guard your hearts and minds through Christ Jesus."

The Spirit of Praise

In all of life's difficulties, God remains faithful, righteous, and loving. Just because we may not receive our 'expected' answers to prayers, the Lord has not forgotten us. We can always find ten thousand reasons to sing His praises!

We are called to introduce all people in this world to the Gospel of Jesus Christ. In the words of St. Francis of Assisi, the Italian saint, poet, and preacher who led a life of poverty: "Preach the Gospel at all times, and when necessary, use words."

Becoming 'living epistles' is possible only through the Holy Spirit-led life, when we surrender ourselves to God. He will never leave us nor forsake us. May we continue to sing His praise unending and may our lives testify to the fact that He is faithful to preserve our souls!

2

TRANSFORMED
BY GRACE

In 1987, an IRA bomb buried Gordon Wilson and his twenty-year-old daughter beneath five feet of rubble. Gordon alone survived. Amazingly, he forgave those who were responsible for the bombing, saying: "I have lost my daughter, but I bear no grudge. I shall pray every night, that God will forgive them." His words caught the media's ears, and even in his grief, the world got a glimpse of grace.

We are to emulate our Lord Jesus Christ, to be people full of grace and wisdom. In pursuit of becoming a God-inspired epistle, each of us needs to be filled with godly wisdom and be guided by His grace, just as Jesus was.

> *"And the child (Jesus) grew and became strong; he was filled with wisdom, and the grace of God was on him."*
>
> *Luke 2:40*

What is grace? It is the unmerited favour we receive from God. Without an understanding of grace, we may strive hard to earn God's favour. But as the apostle Paul wrote, it is not our good works that save us—it is God's grace! (Romans 11:6).

The Gift of Grace

Grace is the church's great distinctive attribute. Philip Yancey writes: "It's the one thing the world cannot duplicate, and the one thing it craves above all else—for only grace can bring hope and transformation to a jaded world."[1]

Grace is a gift from God. When I receive a gift from someone, it is not because I *deserve* this priceless gift—it is simply given to me out of *love*. So it is with God. His grace is given to us, and it is all-sufficient. In 2 Corinthians we read,

> *"And He (Jesus) said to me (the apostle Paul), 'My grace is sufficient for you, for My strength is made perfect in weakness.' Therefore most gladly I will rather boast in my infirmities, that the power of Christ may rest upon me."*
> *2 Corinthians 12:8*

Let us remember that God's grace is available to all, and we are to accept it without any analysis of how we received it or any other baseless questions. It is available to those who are good and not so good, humble and not so humble, passive and not so passive, efficient and not so efficient. It is a gift from God!

The Fruit of Grace: Humility

In the Scriptures, we find this point of difference: when the wicked are shown grace, they do not learn righteousness. Isaiah 26:10 says that "even in a land of uprightness they continue doing evil and do not regard the Lord's majesty and power."

---

1 Taken from *What's So Amazing About Grace?* by Philip Yancey, published by Zondervan, 2002

It is a timely reminder for us that whatever good works we may do, they are not going to earn us our salvation. Salvation is exclusively from God through Christ Jesus. It is by His grace. The apostle Paul emphasises humility when he speaks to the Romans saying,

> *"For by the grace given me I say to every one of you: Do not think of yourself more highly than you ought, but rather think of yourself with sober judgment, in accordance with the faith God has distributed to each of you."*
>
> *Romans 12:3*

We must be humble enough to recognise that, whether we measure up or fall short, God's grace is always freely available. No matter what, we should always return to Him. The Scripture encourages us in this manner: "God opposes the proud but shows favour to the humble" (James 4:6 NLT).

The Cost of Grace

It is one thing to understand that God's gift of grace is free and undeserved, and it's another thing entirely to understand that we have received this grace through Christ's death on the cross, and his glorious resurrection.

The gift of salvation is not like the sin that caused our downfall. According to Romans 5:15-18,

> *". . . the free gift is not like the offense. For if by the one man's offense many died, much more the grace of God and the gift by the grace of the one Man, Jesus Christ, abounded to many . . . Therefore, as through one man's offense judgment came to all men, resulting in condemnation, even so through one*

Man's righteous act the free gift came to all men, resulting in justification of life."

Grateful for Grace

Many people struggle to understand the concept of grace. Surprisingly, even within the church, many believers find it difficult to connect God's grace with the world around them. God's grace is free and cannot be earned. But we need to understand that appreciating God's grace goes beyond just accepting it; it's about recognizing our own need for it first. The deeper our realization of this need, the greater our joy in experiencing His grace.

Let me draw a parallel here: say we compare two children living in two different homes. One child is lavished with goodies every day by his or her parents. The second child lives in a home with adequate food each day but experiences the joy of receiving goodies once a week or a fortnight. Which child is more likely to appreciate the goodies? The second child, of course!

My point is this: it is easy to become complacent about God's grace in our everyday lives because it is so constant and abundant. Let us not become 'accustomed to grace' and focus on our problems rather than counting God's blessings.

Transformed by Grace

When we begin to appreciate this gift from God and realise that we do not deserve the grace He lavishes upon us, our entire perspective changes. God's grace empowers us to understand that we are God's children, created in His image. We are fearfully and wonderfully made (Psalm 139:14). We are kings and priests and a holy nation (1 Peter 2:9-12). We are the apple of His eye (Psalm 17:8). We are overcomers and not a failure (1 John 5:4). We are called to be the light and salt of the world (Matthew 5:13-16).

Hence, the promises in God's word become a reality to us. Take, for example, the promise, "No weapon formed against you will prosper" (Isaiah 54:17). This verse does not say that no weapon will be formed against us, but that no weapon will *prosper* against us. There are many other promises that God has for us, spoken through His people.

How wonderful that our inheritance is linked to God's promises! Galatians 3:18 says,

> *"For if the inheritance depends on the law, then it no longer depends on the promise; but God in His grace gave it to Abraham through a promise."*

Not only that, but according to Romans 4:16, God's promises are for us all!

> *"Therefore, the promise comes by faith, so that it may be by grace and may be guaranteed to all Abraham's offspring—not only to those who are of the law but also to those who have the faith of Abraham. He is the father of us all."*

Responding to Grace

What do we do with this grace that we have lavishly received from God? Here are three responses God is looking for:

1. We are to share God's grace

We help others experience God's grace by passing it on. When we graciously forgive others, overlook their limitations, and lavish love on those who hate us or do not wish us well, our response will make a positive impact on them. We need to be in a state of mind or understanding that God's grace is all-sufficient for us in our daily walk. It is to be shared always, and will be replenished by 'more of His grace' so we can share with many more! As Hebrews 4:16 says, "Let us then approach God's throne of grace with confidence, so that we may receive mercy and find grace to help us in our time of need."

2. We are to testify of God's grace

God's grace gives us the power to testify to God's salvation through our Lord Jesus Christ. In Acts 4:33 we read, "With great power the apostles continued to testify to the resurrection of the Lord Jesus. And God's grace was so powerfully at work in them all."

3. We are to serve with grace

Grace enables us to serve one another. 1 Peter 4:10 says, "We have different gifts given to us according to God's grace. Each of us should use whatever gift we have received to serve others, as faithful stewards of God's grace in its various forms."

As we have received this grace or "unmerited favour from God", we need to step out of our comfort zones and our self-deprecating mentality and move on to be a blessing to others, sharing our story, our life's testimony, and being willing to exercise the gifts God has so graciously given to us. Will we choose to 'become' what God wants us to be?

I have come to realise that it is only by God's grace that I am able to share this message with you. It took me quite some time to fully grasp that God's grace is a gift that is available to everyone, including myself. I accepted this truth with humility, and in response, I let God know that I was ready to share His love with others through that same grace.

Let us respond to His gracious call, setting aside all fear, anxiety and hesitation, and taking that first step of faith. May we say, "Lord, I am available to be used as a channel of Your grace, giving it freely to others and trusting that You will replenish me each time I obey."

3

—

THE PATH OF
WISDOM

On a human level, wisdom is *the judicious application of knowledge*. Wisdom is also the comprehension of what is true, coupled with optimum judgment to act.

Wisdom brings a deep understanding and perception of people, ideas and situations, allowing us to assess and act with discernment. It requires control of our emotional reactions so that universal principles, reason and knowledge prevail to determine our actions.

Wisdom is mostly connected to or deemed to be a friend of those who have achieved merit or excellence according to the world's standards or expectations. It is sought after by academics and is often named as a prayer request for those sitting examinations and tests—unfortunately, it is also easily forgotten when people pass out of school or academic institutions. Wisdom is also associated with the elderly, on account of their many years of life experience and service rendered.

Is achieving merit according to worldly standards the only purpose for wisdom? Will growing in years bring about wisdom that can change people? Why do the wise of this world sometimes become self-centred and feed their ego? Why do some give up pursuing wisdom? Is it because they feel incompetent? Are they comparing themselves with those who have achieved something in life? Do they feel that they don't measure up?

The Source of Wisdom

The Bible has much to say on the topic of wisdom. James 1:5 says:

> "If any of you lacks wisdom, let him ask of God, who gives to all liberally and without reproach, and it will be given to him."

God gives wisdom generously to all who ask!

Interestingly, the 'fear of the Lord' is described as the place where wisdom begins (Proverbs 9:10). This phrase, the fear of the Lord, is not meant to be understood as being fierce in nature. It is simply a reverential attitude to God and a commitment to walk in His ways.

The Safety of Wisdom

In the Old Testament, God directed His people to follow His instructions. God wanted His people to know their choices and behaviour had consequences—sometimes for blessing and sometimes for harm. God's wisdom was a safeguard for them, protecting them from threats and ensuring they would be established and prosper in the earth.

Many times, the people of God were 'stiff-necked' or stubborn, refusing to live according to His ways. Rather than forcing them to obey Him, God allowed them to face the consequences of their actions, much like a parent allows their child to experience the fallout of their own decisions. Of course, it grieves God to watch His children learn the hard way'that His ways are best. How He longed to gather His people like a hen would gather her chicks under its wings! (Matthew 23:37). Nevertheless, His love was always there to restore them, and time and time again He brought them back to Himself. But like so many today, His people did not understand His heart and preferred to lean on their own wisdom. If only they had chosen the reverential fear of God, who is the source of all wisdom.

The Wisdom of the Cross

God's wisdom is greater than the wisdom of the world. The apostle Paul, one of the most learned men of his time, understood that to preach the gospel is to preach the cross of Christ.

> *"For Christ did not send me to baptize, but to preach the gospel, not with eloquent wisdom of words, lest the cross of Christ should be made of no effect."*
> *1 Corinthians 1:17*

How could Paul preach such a Gospel? Because he knew that while the message of the cross is foolishness in the world's eyes, it reveals the power *and wisdom* of God.

> *"For the message of the cross is foolishness to those who are perishing, but to us who are being saved it is the*

power of God. For it is written: 'I will destroy the wisdom of the wise, And bring to nothing the understanding of the prudent.' Where is the wise? Where is the scribe? Where is the disputer of this age? Has not God made foolish the wisdom of this world? For since, in the wisdom of God, the world through wisdom did not know God, it pleased God through the foolishness of the message preached to save those who believe. For Jews request a sign, and Greeks seek after wisdom; but we preach Christ crucified, to the Jews a stumbling block and to the Greeks foolishness, but to those who are called, both Jews and Greeks, Christ the power of God and the wisdom of God. Because the foolishness of God is wiser than men, and the weakness of God is stronger than men."
          1 Corinthians 1:18–25

The message here is loud and clear: The cross of Christ and the grace of God on us reveals the wisdom of God, which is above every other wisdom.

"For you see your calling, brethren, that not many wise according to the flesh, not many mighty, not many noble, are called. But God has chosen the foolish things of the world to put to shame the wise, and God has chosen the weak things of the world to put to shame the things which are mighty; and the base things of the world and the things which are despised God has chosen, and the things which are not, to bring to nothing the things that are, that no flesh should glory in His presence. But of Him you are in Christ Jesus, who became for us wisdom from God—and righteousness and sanctification and

redemption—that, as it is written, 'He who glories, let him glory in the LORD.'"

1 Corinthians 1:26-31

It is the one thing of which the apostle boasts—that he and his fellow leaders conducted themselves with integrity and godly sincerity by the grace of God and not with worldly wisdom.

"Now this is our boast! Our conscience testifies that we have conducted ourselves in the world, and especially in our relations with you, with integrity and godly sincerity. We have done so, relying not on worldly wisdom but on God's grace."

2 Corinthians 1:12 NIV

Growing in Grace and Wisdom

In Scripture, we read that a child should grow in wisdom and in the grace of God. We see this exemplified in the life of the prophet Samuel (1 Samuel 2:26) and our Lord Jesus Christ:

"And the Child grew and became strong in spirit, filled with wisdom; and the grace of God was upon Him."

Luke 2:40

We need to understand the connection between the grace of God and wisdom. The grace of God is the only attribute that initiates, sustains and sets wisdom in motion in our lives. As believers, we have the ability to learn about and know God, thanks to His grace.

How can we grow in grace? Here are three important keys:

1. **Read the Bible.** The Scriptures depict the wisdom and character of God.

2. **Abide in Christ.** The Holy Spirit within us enables us to feel the 'pulse' or heartbeat of God. As we allow the brokenness around us to touch our hearts, as it touches His, we become a conduit of His compassion and healing.

3. **Obey the voice of God.** When we listen to God's voice and obey His call on our lives, we become participants in His greater purposes. Freely giving what we receive from the Lord involves sharing the gospel message and operating in the power of the Holy Spirit to see people healed of sicknesses, restored from brokenness, and delivered from bondage.

Bishop Desmond Tutu said, "Do your little bit of good where you are; it's those little bits of good put together that overwhelm the world." As we grow in the grace of God and become increasingly sensitive to the promptings of the Holy Spirit, we begin to share His heart for this hurting world. The apostle Paul wrote:

> *"Let your conversation be always full of grace, seasoned with salt, so that you may know how to answer everyone."*
> *Colossians 4:6 NIV*

Gifts of Wisdom

We learn from Scripture that as we receive Jesus Christ, God's only Son, into our lives, we are empowered by His Holy Spirit. The Holy Spirit enables us to possess two incredible gifts: the word of wisdom and the word of knowledge. These are very much essential in our daily walk as disciples of Jesus Christ.

> *". . . for to one is given the word of wisdom through the Spirit, to another the word of knowledge through the same*

Spirit, to another faith by the same Spirit, to another gifts of healings by the same Spirit, to another the working of miracles, to another prophecy, to another discerning of spirits, to another different kinds of tongues, to another the interpretation of tongues."
                           1 Corinthians 12:8–10

Let us participate in God's plan with the help of His wisdom powered by His grace.

"So, you also, when you have done everything you were told to do, should say, 'We are unworthy servants; we have only done our duty.'"
                                   Luke 17:10

In doing so, we declare that all glory and power belong to our Lord Jesus Christ and Him alone.

4

THE JOY OF
RIGHTEOUS
LIVING

Just imagine a world dictated by a human definition of righteous living. Such an arbitrary standard would lead to chaos. In the words of Isaiah 64:6 (NIV):

> *"All of us have become like one who is unclean, and all our righteous acts are like filthy rags; we all shrivel up like a leaf, and like the wind our sins sweep us away."*

The truth is, no one born of the flesh can boast of being righteous. Praise God that our righteousness is found in Christ! It is therefore imperative that we understand our position in the Righteous One.

Our Position in Christ

What is our position concerning righteousness? We are made righteous through our Lord and Saviour Jesus Christ because of His death on the cross and His resurrection.

Scripture tells us:

> *"We are therefore Christ's ambassadors, as though God were making His appeal through us. We implore you on Christ's behalf: Be reconciled to God. God made Him who had no sin to be sin for us, so that in him we might become the righteousness of God."*
>
> *2 Corinthians 5:20–21*

We cannot be made righteous through our own efforts. Instead, we are made righteous through Christ's faithfulness. Through Him, we have "peace with God through our Lord Jesus Christ" (Romans 5:1–11). Instead of focussing on our 'works' or 'worthiness', we are to take our place in the Lord Jesus, who is our righteousness (Hebrews 12:1–2). Nevertheless, the Bible describes some characteristics of someone who God considers 'righteous'.

Righteousness in the Old Testament

In the book of Ezekiel, we see the Lord dealing with the people of Israel. The nation of Israel had seen the great deeds He had done in their midst, yet they were not willing to turn their lives around for good. God implored His people to live according to His ways and not according to the ways of the nations around them, or of their ancestors.

> *". . . even if these three men—Noah, Daniel and Job— were in it, they could save only themselves by their righteousness, declares the Sovereign Lord."*
>
> *Ezekiel 14:14*

Let us consider the three men who are described as 'righteous' in the Old Testament: Noah, Daniel, and Job. Noah and his family were saved from the flood that wiped out all other inhabitants. Daniel and his friends went through the lions' den and fire respectively and were not affected by it. Job experienced pain, loss and grief, but did not give up and was rewarded a double portion. All three of these men were rewarded at the end of their periods of trial. Their close walk with Jehovah (God Almighty) brought about these dramatic results.

God was willing to spare the residents of Sodom and Gomorrah if there were a few righteous and God-fearing people there. He gave time for everyone living in Sodom and Gomorrah to repent and turn to Him. God valued the efforts of these men to live righteously, but we must remember that this should have been everyone's natural response to a Holy God. One man's righteousness could not be transferred to someone else.

Righteousness in the New Testament

Let us look at the exemplary life of Zacharias and Elizabeth. This man and woman were both "righteous before God, walking in all the commandments and ordinances of the Lord blameless" (Luke 1:6). God, in His mercy, acknowledges their righteousness, and in response, entrusts them to be the parents of John the Baptist, the one who would prepare the way for the Lord Jesus.

God is willing to make use of you and me in this world. Are we making ourselves available by living a righteous life that is set apart for His glorious work? In pursuing a righteous and godly life, with the assistance of the Holy Spirit, we would make room for God to heal, deliver and restore us. Look at the following verses:

1. God heals

"Confess your trespasses to one another, and pray for one another, that you may be healed. The effective, fervent prayer of a righteous man avails much."
James 5:16

2. God delivers

"Moses answered the people, 'Do not be afraid. Stand firm and you will see the deliverance the Lord will bring you today. The Egyptians you see today you will never see again.'"
Exodus 14:13

3. God restores

"O my God, incline Your ear and hear; open Your eyes and see our desolations, and the city which is called by Your name; for we do not present our supplications before You because of our righteous deeds, but because of Your great mercies."
Daniel 9:18

Wisdom and Righteousness

If we demonstrate wisdom, living godly lives, we can bless the world by preventing others from their folly.

"The righteous and the wise and their works are in the hand of God. People know neither love nor hatred by anything they see before them."
Ecclesiastes 9:1

The bottom line is, despite our unrighteousness, God is always merciful. Romans 9:15 says:

> *"I will have mercy on whom I have mercy, and I will have compassion on whom I have compassion."*

God does not hold our sins against us. He has made a way for us all to be righteous in His sight. Jesus Christ secured our righteousness by His obedience to the Law, living a sinless life. This righteousness is made available to us and is "given through faith in Jesus Christ to all who believe" (Romans 3:22). Apart from Christ, everyone must stand before God in his or her righteousness. Praise God, He has become our righteousness! Let us echo the words of the apostle Paul:

> *"(That I may be) found in Him, not having my own righteousness from the law, but that which is through faith in Christ, the righteousness from God on the basis of faith."*
>
> *Philippians 3:9*

5

—

BORN IS THE KING

At Christmas, over seven billion people observe, hear, talk about, or participate in, the celebration of Jesus' birth. Of course, not everyone understands the great Advent that took place two thousand or more years ago. Nevertheless, Christmas is a time of festivity and a time to get together, with sumptuous food and celebrations.

For those of us who dearly love our Lord and Saviour Jesus Christ, Christmas is seen as the time in history when God reconciled mankind to Himself. We also understand that it is the season of fulfilment of prophecies that were spoken centuries ago.

> "For a child is born to us, a son is given to us. The government will rest on His shoulders. And He will be called: Wonderful Counselor, Mighty God, Everlasting Father, Prince of Peace. His government and its peace will never end. He will rule with fairness and justice from the throne of His ancestor David for all eternity. The

passionate commitment of the Lord of Heaven's Armies will make this happen!"

Isaiah 9:6–7 NLT

The Significance of Jesus' Birth

The joy that Christmas brings to us is like that of a child being born into our family. It's a time of reconciliation between families and friends. Hurts are healed and relationships are renewed. Amidst storms and raging global challenges like war and strife, the peace that Christmas brings is built on the assurance that our Lord and Saviour Jesus Christ is with us even during the turbulence of life.

Not only that, but there is great significance in the coming of Christ, the righteous Son of God, as a human baby. The apostle Paul wrote:

> *"He made Himself of no reputation, taking the form of a bondservant, and coming in the likeness of men."*
>
>
>
> *Philippians 2:7*
>
>

In coming as a human, Jesus showed us the righteousness of God *and* is able to impart to each one of us the righteousness of God.

God's Unconditional Love

This love that we cherish during Christmas is the uncondi-tional love of our faithful and immutable heavenly Father. His love is a healing balm, soothing all our hurts and pain. His *agape* love, the highest form of the love of God for human beings, gives us the strength to move forward, even to the extent of loving those who have wronged us.

As we exchange gifts and express love for one another in various ways, let us consider and ask ourselves: *Are we experiencing Christ's love more and more in our lives? Are we taking steps of faith to experience more of His love?*

The Father's love—from the manger to the cross of Calvary and to the throne—can only be grasped as we continue to walk closely with Him every day.

Understanding God's Love

As those who dwell within the Shepherd's fold, we all have differing experiences and understanding of Christ's love. And yet each one of us is experiencing His love at this very moment!

How can we grow to understand the entire length, depth and height of His love? To a certain extent, we can understand the Father's love from the broad perspective of the manger and even Calvary's cross. John 3:16 sums it up:

> *"For God so loved the world that He gave His only begotten Son, that whoever believes in Him should not perish but have everlasting life."*

Yes, it will take more than a lifetime to comprehend His love for us!

How can we understand the Father's love from the perspective of His throne in our current circumstances? There are legitimate questions raised by many: *Why does evil continue to raise its nasty head? How can a loving God allow innocent people and children to suffer?*

The easy response to these questions is that we will only know the answers when we get to heaven. What we do know is what the apostle Paul wrote in his letter to the Romans. He was convinced that nothing and no one could separate us from His love (Romans 8:31–39). This is an attribute of Christ's love: it is all-encompassing.

The Call to Share His Love

There is no greater measure of love than that the sinless Christ should suffer and die on account of our sins. History has recorded the brutal death of our Lord and Saviour Jesus Christ at Calvary. Our heavenly Father permitted His Son to go through this gruesome experience, simply because He loves all humanity and longs to share in our suffering.

But that is not the end of the story. As "joint heirs with Christ", we know that when we suffer with Him, we will also be "glorified together with Him" (Romans 8:17).

All of us have a mission to spread the good news that Jesus died for all humanity. This world would be a better place if everyone embraced the love of the Father as revealed in and through His Son, our Lord and Saviour Jesus Christ. What are we waiting for?! No wonder Jesus said, "The harvest is plentiful but the workers are few" (Matthew 9:37 NIV). Our heavenly Father is calling every one of us to take a step of faith, to not only understand more of His love but to share it with everyone.

As those who are joined to Him and made complete with all the fullness of life and power that comes from Him, let us invite others also to be joined to Him and to share in our Father's love. We are called to be His ambassadors of love, peace, and joy. John records how Jesus breathed on His disciples and said, "Receive the Holy Spirit" (John 20:22). The good news is that we are equipped to be ambassadors for Christ because we have the Holy Spirit in us, enabling us to do "greater works" for the expansion of God's Kingdom in the lives of people around us.

Ministering the Love of the Father

I would love nothing more than to see God working through us today as He did in the Book of Acts. Of course, God is working and carrying out His plan through many of us. We are a blessing to our families, communities and nations when God uses us to be channels of His never-ending resources. What would it be like if the whole world experienced God's healing touch, received the encouragement it needs in these chaotic times, and enjoyed the peace of Christ that passes all understanding?

Christmas should be a season for all to be encouraged, healed, supported, renewed, and loved. As Mother Teresa, the founder of Missionaries of Charity, once said: "It is Christmas every time you let God love others through you."

May we celebrate the season of Christmas knowing that we are His chosen vessels of hope, and ambassadors of peace in this world.

6

——

THE MESSAGE OF RECONCILIATION

In the Gospels, the birth of Christ ushers in the accomplishment of God's plan through the life, death, resurrection and ascension of His Son. God the Father loved us, His created ones, so much that He wanted nothing more than to reconcile us to Himself. He achieved this by sending His one and only Son into the world to go through agony at Calvary and to die for us. The Book of Romans says:

> *"While we were God's enemies we were reconciled to him through the death of his Son."*
>
> *Romans 5:10*

Even though our reconciliation meant the sacrifice of His Son for us, praise God!—our Lord and Saviour Jesus Christ conquered death by rising from the tomb on the third day.

The Restoration of All Creation

God the Father *planned* to send His Son to die so that all mankind might be reconciled to Himself. We see this in the words of Caiaphas, the high priest at the time of Jesus' death, who prophesied that Jesus would die not only for Israel but also for all the children of God:

> *"And one of them, Caiaphas, being high priest that year, said to them, 'You know nothing at all, nor do you consider that it is expedient for us that one man should die for the people, and not that the whole nation should perish.' Now this he did not say on his own authority; but being high priest that year he prophesied that Jesus would die for the nation, and not for that nation only, but also that He would gather together in one the children of God who were scattered abroad."*
>
> *John 11:49–52*

Our Response to Christ's Sacrifice

The apostle Paul, in his message to the Corinthians, emphasises the importance of our response to His great initiative of reconciliation (2 Corinthians 5:17–21).

Reconciling with God is our response to Him as He draws near to us. We need to make every effort to establish a growing relationship with Him. It is an active response; one that goes beyond our emotions and feelings. It requires us to break free from our inhibitions and barriers. Our response is an overflow of what He has accomplished for us.

When we become reconciled to God, we become Christ's ambassadors. As Christ's resident representatives in this world, we have the responsibility of furthering God's interests toward the restoration of His creation.

Christ's Resident Representatives

If we are to represent God's interests, we need to know the plans God has in store for us and the people around us. Understanding His plan for us includes taking stock of our present situation and looking for opportunities around us. It requires us to break free from the doubts, inhibitions, fears and limitations that keep us from participating in God's plan.

We begin to experience the fullness of joy in Jesus Christ as we step out in faith. This can be as simple as praying for someone in need in the quietness of our homes as the Holy Spirit brings that person to our remembrance. As we start to obey His still small voice, the Holy Spirit will teach us and help us to share God's plans for others. Let us, with all earnestness, desire to step into greater things for God.

> *"Therefore, my dear brothers and sisters, stand firm. Let nothing move you. Always give yourselves fully to the work of the Lord, because you know that your labour in the Lord is not in vain."*
>
> *1 Corinthians 15:58*

Overcomers in this World

When we are at peace with God, He helps us overcome the challenges of the world. John writes:

> *"Everyone born of God overcomes the world. This is the victory that has overcome the world, even our faith."*
>
> *1 John 5:4 NIV*

This is God's promise: we will become overcomers amid challenges. We will have peace during any storm we may encounter—strained relationships, tough situations, sickness, or sorrow. We will be protected from the darts of the enemy as our thoughts, words, and actions are brought under the leading of the Holy Spirit. We will also be able to wait on God without becoming anxious, angry, or impatient.

James 1:2–4 (The Message) encourages us,

> *"Consider it a sheer gift, friends, when tests and challenges come at you from all sides. You know that under pressure, your faith-life is forced into the open and shows its true colours. So don't try to get out of anything prematurely. Let it do its work so you become mature and well-developed, not deficient in any way."*

Whatever our present situation may be, we can rest in the fact that our God is sovereign and He knows it all. In Him, there is hope, love, and peace that surpasses all understanding. Because of this, we can be "filled to the measure of all the fullness of God" (Ephesians 3:19). Let us never forget the immeasurable love of God for us in Christ.

> *"Greater love has no one than this: to lay down one's life for one's friends."*
>
> *John 15:13 NIV*

7

ENCOUNTERS
WITH GOD

Isn't it interesting that some of our deepest encounters with the Lord happen amidst our greatest challenges and disappointments? When things are difficult, it is easy to place the blame on Him, our circumstances, or others. Seldom do we realise that our difficulties are an opportunity to encounter the sovereign Lord of the universe. If we wish to have an encounter with the Lord, we must learn to recognise His presence in our trials and respond with faith and trust.

Simon Peter's Encounter

"[Jesus] said to Simon, 'Launch out into the deep and let down your nets for a catch.' But Simon answered and said to Him, 'Master, we have toiled all night and caught nothing; nevertheless, at Your word I will let down the net.' And when they had done this, they caught a great number of fish, and their net was breaking. So they signaled to their partners in the other boat to come and help them. And they came and filled both the boats, so that they began to sink. When Simon Peter saw it, he fell

*down at Jesus' knees, saying, 'Depart from me, for I am a
sinful man, O Lord!'"*

Luke 5:4–8

Simon Peter was going about his daily business when he
experienced a miracle beyond his understanding. A seasoned
fisherman, he obeyed Jesus' command to cast his net into deep
waters, even though he hadn't caught anything the whole
night. Similarly, when Jesus meets us in our life situations in a
way that exceeds our expectations and skills, we can recognise
it as an encounter with God.

Peter's response shows us that he recognised Jesus as
extraordinary. He felt his unworthiness and was willing to
follow Him immediately.

Paul's Encounter

*"But rise and stand on your feet; for I have appeared
to you for this purpose, to make you a minister and a
witness both of the things which you have seen and of the
things which I will yet reveal to you."*

Acts 26:16

The apostle Paul's encounter was different. Paul thought that
persecuting Christians was right and just—until he met Jesus
Christ on the road to Damascus. Similarly, we might believe
we have figured things out and continue to do them in our
own way, following our usual routine—until we encounter
God in a most unexpected manner!

We see in Paul's response how he was obedient to God's call.
He accepted God's plan for him immediately without any

defiance and was willing to go through many trials, hardships and persecution on account of following Jesus Christ.

An Encounter at the Pool of Bethesda

"He said to him, 'Do you want to be made well?' The sick man answered Him, 'Sir, I have no man to put me into the pool when the water is stirred up; but while I am coming, another steps down before me.' Jesus said to him, 'Rise, take up your bed and walk.' And immediately the man was made well, took up his bed, and walked."

John 5:6–9

The man at the pool of Bethesda could only respond to Jesus by narrating his inability to step into the pool on his own. If only he had been able to respond instantly and say, "Yes, I want to be made well!" The man did not know who was talking to him. However, once he was healed, he was eager to let others know who had healed him! It is strange, however, that we do not hear about this man again. I wonder if he missed the opportunity to get to know Jesus better, to follow Him and learn more from Jesus?

Let us not be satisfied with hearing about someone else's experience with God. When it comes to encountering God, let us always seek a first-hand experience. Jesus *invites* us to follow Him; He will never force it on us. He waits patiently for us to recognise His encounters and extends an invitation to follow Him. He may not be calling all of us into full-time ministry or mission work, but He is calling us all to be salt and light in this world and to draw more people to Christ.

"You are the salt of the earth; but if the salt loses its flavor, how shall it be seasoned? It is then good for nothing but to be thrown out and trampled underfoot by men. You are the light of the world. A city that is set on a hill cannot be hidden."

Matthew 5:13–14

As those who have encountered Jesus Christ, we are healed of brokenness, freed from all sin and unrighteousness, and empowered by the Holy Spirit. What a wonderful position to impact others and lead them to Christ!

8

—

OUR
INTERDEPENDENCE

As believers, we are to understand that we are dependent on one another. Just like our triune God—God the Father, God the Son and God the Holy Spirit—we have distinctive identities, but we are interdependent. We function as individual persons but work together in unison for a purpose. Genesis 1:26 tells us that the Father, Son and Holy Spirit were involved in creating mankind in their image and likeness. This relational dependence is a principle that has been established in heaven and extended to us on earth. The Trinity is our example of a perfectly functioning, interdependent relationship.

As humans, we are created to live in community while keeping in step with God's guidance. In other words, we are to depend on God and on each other as human beings. Ideally, this interdependence is seen in the family unit, community, city, nation, and the world. Hebrews 10:23–25 says:

". . . let us consider how we may spur one another on toward love and good deeds, not giving up meeting together, as some are in the habit of doing, but

encouraging one another—and all the more as you see the Day approaching."

Relational Interdependence

Interdependence should be seen both in the physical and spiritual realms.

1. Physical Realm

The reality is that as humans, we need each other. Our existence on this planet earth requires us to function as individuals, while at the same time to nurture our relationships with our Creator and with one another. In the words of 1 John 1:3:

"We proclaim to you what we have seen and heard, so that you also may have fellowship with us. And our fellowship is with the Father and with his Son, Jesus Christ."

The Bible gives plenty of examples of people living in dependence on God and in interdependence with His people. Consider these Scriptures:

- God created Eve as a helper for Adam (Genesis 2:20–22)
- The walls of Jericho were brought down by the Lord, but the Israelites had to work in coordination with each other and each group had a role to play (Joshua 6)
- The prophet Elijah had to depend on a widow for a meal (1 Kings 17)
- The Shunammite woman had to depend on the prophet Elisha to bring her son back to life (2 Kings 4:8–38)
- The believers prayed for Peter when he was in chains and the prison was shaken (Acts 12:5)

As we become aware of our need for God and each other, we will become sensitive to the needs around us and make ourselves available for others spontaneously. This, I believe, is the prompting of the Holy Spirit in us.

2. Spiritual Realm

The spiritual realm is where we most clearly see God the Father, God the Son and God the Holy Spirit interacting with each other to accomplish their plans and purposes on earth. Mary, the mother of Jesus, was required to carry our Lord and Saviour Jesus Christ as a baby in her womb to fulfil God's plan to reveal Himself to this world in the form of a human being (Matthew 1:18; Luke 1:26–38).

As the Son of God, Jesus came into this world so that we could be called God's sons and daughters (Galatians 3:26). We are also called to be His friends (John 15:15). The Lord reveals His plans to His friends. God also reveals His thoughts through men and women (Amos 4:13). God speaks in prophetic words through men with the help of the Holy Spirit (2 Peter 1:21). The Holy Spirit loves to speak directly to a person about his or her future, but He also speaks through friends and family and those in ministry for that person's blessing, encouragement or guidance. Either way, God is wanting to communicate with us. As God's people, we enjoy such a wonderful relationship with our Creator!

When we realise that our God always wants to have a relationship with us and communicate with us directly or through His people, we should make it our aim to strengthen our relationship with Him and to be a channel of His communication to others.

Practicing Interdependence

Having understood the principle of interdependence, let us embrace community living in a practical way. Here are some ways we can do that:

- Continue meeting together, spurring one another toward love and good deeds, and encouraging one another.
- Demonstrate unity and peace with fellow Christians. As brothers and sisters in Christ, we are called to be united in the Spirit by the grace of our Lord Jesus Christ. The Apostle Paul urges us to agree with one another, avoid divisions, and be perfectly united in mind and thought (1 Corinthians 1:10).
- When we receive blessings, we must not become selfish. When wealth increases, we must not shift our focus on it. Instead, we are to uphold the cause of the fatherless, the widows, the destitute, and the orphans. Let us be quick to meet the needs around us (Psalm 62:10; Isaiah 1:17).
- Refrain from condemning or judging others. When we are self-righteous and quick to judge, we can easily miss the opportunity our Lord gives us to reconcile with His people. Let us be mindful that within the body of Christ, we need to build up and encourage one another to be a blessing.
- Demonstrate gratitude to our heavenly Father for the people He has placed in our lives—those who have helped us in times of physical need, spoken words of encouragement and prophecy, prayed for healing, and many more.
- We should always be aware that every member of the body of Christ is important, whether a spiritual leader,

43

evangelist, Christian friend, layperson, young or old, rich or poor. Let us take care of the people who serve God, and be mindful of the time and effort they have sown into our lives (Galatians 6:10). No one can be considered dispensable in the kingdom of God. Every one of us is valuable (Acts 21:17–20).

As we walk on this earth, let us be reminded that we need relationships with one another and that interdependence is a key principle within God's Kingdom. Let us always think of others as better than ourselves. The Lord has designed us from the beginning and intricately knitted and blended us with variety and colour, as a masterpiece, to fulfil His good purpose (Ecclesiastes 3:11).

The Christian life is a life of repentance, faith, and good works lived through the power of the Holy Spirit. By grace, let us be conformed to the image of Christ to the glory of God.

"May the God of all comfort and peace rule our hearts, as we present ourselves as a living sacrifice to Him, a pleasing aroma acceptable unto Him."
                                                    Romans 12:1

As those who have been blessed beyond measure, may we be a channel of blessing to many, and may we offer our lives in service, knowing that our brothers and sisters need our personal involvement.

9

—

A CHRIST-CENTRED FAMILY

In His wisdom, God has entrusted men and women with the task of upholding His standards in the family, community and nation. First, He created a man, and from there, he made a woman, who He placed beside the man. From the beginning, God intended that man and woman would share His words and His ways with one another. To Adam, God gave the instruction not to eat from the tree of knowledge of good and evil. In turn, Adam was responsible for communicating this instruction to Eve. When together they disobeyed, God called out to them, "Where are you?" His heart is always for the restoration of our relationship with Him.

Ever since Adam and Eve disobeyed God, pain in toil and in childbearing have become our way of life. Even so, the Lord reserves a threefold blessing for those who are willing to lead his family with Jesus Christ in the centre.

The Lord *communes* with the Christ-centred family, just as He did with Adam and Eve when He visited them in the cool of the evening before they disobeyed Him.

The Lord *confides* His plans for such a family and for those they are associated with, just as He did for Abraham. To Abraham God clearly communicated His intention to bless him with a son. Years later, He gave a clear warning to Sodom and Gomorrah through Abraham.

The Lord *delivers* the Christ-centred family and fights their battles. Though the family may face many troubles, the Lord acts on our behalf and enables us to be overcomers, despite the difficulties that come our way.

Righteousness in the Family

It is reassuring to us in our day and age that God's plan has always been that we and our families would uphold His ways and that we would continue to walk faithfully with Him. Let's look at the example of Noah, Daniel and Job, three men who were commended for their righteousness and experienced God's hand of blessing even in perilous times (Ezekiel 14:14-20).

1.   Liberation in Times of Evil

Noah implicitly followed God's direction and instruction in building an ark that would be for the salvation of his family. Are we prepared to lead our families with such attention to detail? Noah's reverence for God led him to offer a sacrifice on an altar as soon as he and his family were able to leave the ark. No wonder our Lord Jesus Christ referenced Noah's faith when he spoke about the end of the age (Matthew 24:37–38; Luke 18:8). Because of his actions, he was called a "preacher of righteousness" (2 Peter 2:5).

2. Deliverance in Times of Peril

Daniel was a young man who did not hesitate to worship Jehovah and make himself available to God. Whenever God gave a sign or dream to a heathen king, Daniel was willing to interpret it—despite the risk to his life. As a prophet, Daniel was put to the test many times. What does this mean for us? Will we continue to serve God even when it costs us our lives? Daniel faced extreme threats, yet he chose to act in obedience to God.

3. Authority in Times of Testing

Job was known as the greatest man among all the peoples of the east. But although he had much wealth and an abundance of material possessions, he chose to 'stand in the gap', interceding for his children. When disaster struck and all his children, wealth and possessions were destroyed, still Job did not curse God.

Can we also acknowledge that God is the source of all that we have? Can we continue to trust God even when we are faced with disappointments and failures, as Job did? Are we able to stand like Job, submit to the authority of God, and know His purposes are being fulfilled in our lives? Can we testify without the faintest doubt that our God has never let us down?

Our Three-fold Role in the Family

Our Lord Jesus has a threefold office as prophet, priest and king. Likewise, the apostle Paul, in his epistle to the Ephesians, writes that Christ himself gave us *prophets* to equip and build up the body of Christ (Ephesians 4:11–12). In the Book of Revelation, John writes that Christ has made us to be *priests* and *kings* to serve our God and Father. God expects His sons and daughters to perform the same roles in their families.

In order to fulfil our priestly duties in the everyday walk of our lives, we need to reflect on what the Bible says. God expects us to obey Him and keep His requirements so that we can govern His house and have charge over His courts (Zechariah 3:6-7). Like Noah, we need to exercise obedience in faith so that we may be a channel of blessing to our future descendants.

A prophet has revelations of God through visions and dreams. But he must go beyond this experience—like Daniel, a prophet must be bold and courageous to speak without compromise whatever the Lord lays on our hearts.

To live as a king, we need to know the heartbeat of the King of kings. Having the status of a king does not mean simply to have power, wealth, and possessions. It is to live with the awareness that God is the source of everything and that He has the right to use our wealth and possessions for His glory. As kings in the family, we need to be confident that He is our *Jehovah Nissi,* our protector and banner of victory. When the enemy comes at us from all sides, God is our protector, the one who sustains us and all that we have. If we put our trust in our wealth and possessions, we will fail to see God's plan fulfilled through our lives. However, if we put our complete trust in Him, He is faithful to use us and all that we have for His glory.

Are we therefore willing to submit ourselves under the mighty hand of God, so that He will raise us up in due time? Let us be reminded that to be a priest, prophet and king, we need to humbly obey, confidently serve, and know that God is the author and perfecter of our faith. We need to meditate on the truth so that we might stand firm against the darts of the enemy (2 Corinthians 10:5; Romans 8:13).

In doing so, our Lord Jesus will transform us to become fruit-bearing trees—those who bear spiritual fruit in and out of season and are a blessing to those who are lost, discouraged, or entangled in sin. People around us at work and in the community will be drawn to us because of the love, truth and transformational power that flows as we keep our Lord Jesus Christ at the centre of our lives.

10

THE GOD WHO RESPONDS

As we live godly lives in our communities and lead our families in the ways of the Lord, we can be sure that the Lord will respond by sharing His innermost thoughts and desires with us. Psalm 25:14 says that the Lord shares his secrets with and shows His covenant to those who fear Him and revere Him. Likewise, Deuteronomy 29:29 says:

> *"The secret things belong to the Lord our God; but those things which are revealed belong to us and to our children forever, that we may do all the words of this law."*

Those who respect and honour Him, God will admit into the secret place of communion with Himself.

Abraham was such a friend of God. In Genesis, we read:

> *"And the Lord said, 'Shall I hide from Abraham what I am about to do?"*
>
> *Genesis 18:17 NIV*

God calls His children not servants but friends, as he called Abraham. When God revealed what He was about to do to Sodom and Gomorrah, Abraham interceded. As children of God, we know better than others the meaning of His providence and what God is doing with us and others around us. We know by experience the blessings of the covenant and the pleasure of the fellowship we have with the Father and His Son Jesus Christ. This is the priceless honour we have as His children.

In Job 15:8, Eliphaz (Job's friend) asked Job: "Have you heard the secret counsel of God? Do you limit wisdom to yourself?" When we fear and revere the Lord Jehovah, the one true God will reveal His secrets to us through His Holy Spirit. He speaks to us afresh, revealing His plan to us at the right time. Abraham heard God asking him to sacrifice his only son Isaac. At the very last minute, Abraham received a fresh instruction from God not to lay his hand on Isaac, but instead to sacrifice a lamb He had provided (Genesis 22:12).

Since God makes known His plan to us at every point, we are required to tune ourselves to His fresh prompting at all times. We should not stagnate but move forward as we experience Him each day in our lives. Let us meditate further on God's promises and His covenants to us as individuals, families, and communities.

A Covenant-keeping God

God responds to His people by keeping His covenants.

In Genesis 15, God made a covenant with Abraham, and in chapter 18, God affirms His choice. Abraham trusted the Lord to establish His covenant with him by teaching the way of the Lord to his entire household (Genesis 18:19).

In 1 Chronicles 17, God made a covenant with David. God spoke to David through the prophet Nathan and said,

> *"I will be his father, and he will be my son. I will never take my love away from him, as I took it away from your predecessor."*
>
> 1 Chronicles 17:13 NIV

In later life, King David made it clear to his son Solomon that God's promise would be fulfilled if Solomon and his successors walked faithfully before the Lord, referring to the covenant between God and David (1 Kings 2:4).

In Exodus 34, God made a similar covenant with Moses:

> *"I am making a covenant with you. Before all your people I will do wonders never before done in any nation in all the world. The people you live among will see how awesome is the work that I, the Lord, will do for you. Obey what I command you today. I will drive out before you the Amorites, Canaanites, Hittites, Perizzites, Hivites and Jebusites."*
>
> Exodus 34:10–11 NIV

When we receive God's invitation to have a covenant relationship with Him, our response should be to teach and direct our household in His ways and by faith expect God's covenant to be fulfilled in our lives.

Hebrews 11 says that the people listed in that chapter were still living by faith when they died (v. 13). They did not receive the things promised, they only saw them and welcomed them from a distance, admitting that they were foreigners and strangers on earth. We also need to walk by faith and not by sight and believe that God is faithful to His promises.

Love, Authority and Wisdom

The apostle Paul wrote:

> *"Who has known the mind of the Lord so as to instruct him? But we have the mind of Christ."*
>
> *1 Corinthians 2:16 NIV*

In John 7:17, Jesus says:

> *"If anyone wants to do His will, he shall know concerning the doctrine, whether it is from God or whether I speak on My own authority."*

I refer to love, authority and wisdom as 'the three gems' gathered in this life. May the Lord our God help us understand His Word, know the plans that are in His heart, and follow Him diligently with fear and reverence, so that He may establish His covenant with us.

11

THE NATURE OF SUFFERING

Is there an answer to all of life's questions? Where is God when it hurts? Does God permit suffering in our lives? Why does not God intervene in the injustice that we see around the globe? These are some of the questions that both non-Christians and Christians grapple with.

Seeing and Understanding God

God is supreme, and all His thoughts, words and deeds are supernatural. Sometimes we are reluctant to share with others that God is more than able to meet our needs. This may be on account of the suffering and failure that we face in our lives, or because our answer to prayer for the healing of a fellow believer was not as we expected, or is delayed.

When we pray for healing, do we believe that God is *Jehovah Rapha,* the Healer? When we pray for a difficult situation to be removed, do we trust that He is the answer to all our problems in life? Do we pray with confidence, knowing that He will hear our prayer? Or are we reluctant to pray for healing or a change in the situation because we believe God will do what He intends to do whether we pray or not?

The Bible has answers to our questions. The key point is that we must allow the Holy Spirit to reveal His plan to us when we intercede for individuals, families and nations. Then we can pray according to God's will and be confident that our prayers will be answered.

Prayer as a Tool

In obedience to Scripture, let us take our every petition to the Lord in prayer. The apostle Paul wrote:

> "Do not be anxious about anything, but in every situation, by prayer and petition, with thanksgiving, present your requests to God."
>
> Philippians 4:6 NIV

In the Bible, we find many examples of those whose prayers were miraculously answered.

Isaac prayed to the Lord on behalf of his wife because she was childless. The Lord answered his prayer, and Rebekah became pregnant (Genesis 25:21).

The prophet Isaiah delivered a message from the Lord to King Hezekiah that he was going to die. When King Hezekiah heard this, he wept bitterly and prayed to the Lord. Then the Word from the Lord came a second time to Isaiah, instructing the prophet to tell King Hezekiah that the Lord had extended the king's life for fifteen years (2 Kings 20).

Mark 1:35 and Luke 5:16 are distinct references to Jesus' prayer life. We also learn from the four Gospels that Jesus performed many miracles.

Our Lord and Saviour Jesus Christ, the Son of God, always went to His Father in prayer. But Jesus also committed Himself to His Father's will. In Luke 22, Jesus is praying on the Mount of Olives, seeking His Father that He might remove the cup from Him. "Yet not my will, but yours be done," He prayed. As we read on, we understand that Jesus had to go through horrific suffering and consequently faced a painful death for the sake of the redemption of humanity. Jesus Christ obediently and knowingly paid the ultimate price for your and my redemption from sin and eternal death.

Is suffering or failure God's plan for us? No, it is not. Is there an answer to all the questions in life? The answer to this is also "no". Then how do we comprehend and tackle the questions of life? We can only aim to understand life's challenges by walking in close intimacy with our Lord and Saviour Jesus Christ, through the indwelling Holy Spirit.

Intimacy With God

Those who are led by the Holy Spirit are called "children of God", according to Romans 8:14. The indwelling Holy Spirit plays a major role in our prayer life. He "helps us in our weakness", and "intercedes for us through wordless groans" according to the will of God (Romans 8:26–27). He also gives us discernment and sound judgment (1 Corinthians 2:14–16).

We know that suffering and pain are not in God's plan. However, having intimacy with God will help us wade through life with its crises and failures, and be able to tackle them with the right perspective. We need the Holy Spirit to help us to find peace and comfort through dark times.

As we live intimately with God, we become an epistle to the world around us. God intends that our life and faith experience would direct the people we encounter to Christ (2 Corinthians 3:2). When we live with the help and the leading of the Holy Spirit every day, we set an example for others to follow, helping them to come to grips with this life on earth. Let us cultivate intimacy with God early in life. As the apostle Paul instructed Timothy:

> *"Don't let anyone look down on you because you are young, but set an example for the believers in speech, in conduct, in love, in faith and in purity."*
>
> *1 Timothy 4:12 NIV*

Suffering and failure may be part of our lives, but as we ponder on examples from the Bible, the life of our Lord Jesus Christ, and the testimonies of exemplary Christians, we can be overcomers. Let us be encouraged by what Jesus said to His disciples,

> *"These things I have spoken to you, that in Me you may have peace. In the world you will have tribulation; but be of good cheer, I have overcome the world."*
>
> *John 16:33*

12

FACING THE ADVERSARY

To be adequately equipped to face our adversary, we need to take stock of our resources, strategize how we can combat our adversary, and execute those plans at the right time. Our competence in combat or war comes from God (2 Corinthians 3:5–6). We need to be aware that we are the children of the Most High God. The weapons of our warfare are not material, but they are mighty in the Holy Spirit. The power of the resurrected Christ which overcame death is sufficient to bring down the strongholds in our lives when we claim authority in the only name that is high above all names—the name of Jesus Christ.

By definition, an adversary is one that contends with, opposes or resists. It is usually Satan who brings adversity into our lives. The apostle Peter warns us,

> *"Be sober, be vigilant; because your adversary the devil walks about like a roaring lion, seeking whom he may devour. Resist him, steadfast in your faith, knowing that the same sufferings are experienced by your brotherhood in the world."*
>
> *1 Peter 5:8–9*

To face our adversary in the spiritual realm, we need to focus on three important points:

1. Stand firm in the knowledge that our Lord and Saviour Jesus Christ has fought and won the battle for us (1 Corinthians 15:55–57).
2. Allow the Holy Spirit to take control of ourselves and bring forth the fruit and the gifts of the Holy Spirit (Galatians 5:22–23;1 Corinthians 12:8–10).
3. Overcome our adversary by claiming authority over the adversary in the powerful name of our Lord and Saviour, Jesus Christ (Ephesians 1:19–21).

These are ways that help us to operate in the spiritual realm:

1. Develop intimacy with God by keeping our focus on Him, reading the Bible, talking to Him, and being with Him. Experiencing intimacy with God gives us the knowledge and understanding of the resources we possess.
2. Yield our lives to the Holy Spirit for Him to effectively enable us to live wisely. The Holy Spirit motivates us to live a life pleasing to God. He equips us with gifts and the fruit of the Spirit (Hebrews 13:21).
3. Use the name of our Lord and Saviour Jesus Christ when confronted (2 Timothy 3:16–17). Power is available in the name of Christ Jesus to His children and to all those who earnestly seek divine help. The power that raised Jesus Christ from the dead is the same yesterday, today and forever, and is available to us as we call upon His name (Mark 16:17–18).

Discerning the Adversary

The apostle Paul clearly identifies his many adversaries and makes use of the resources he possesses to wage warfare. He wrote, "For a great and effective door has opened to me, and there are many adversaries" (1 Corinthians 16:9).

Adversaries are often present when we have fallen short of what God intended to do in and through us, or when we are at the brink of a breakthrough. If you have waited on the Lord and are sure that you are indeed heading in the right direction, press on despite the setbacks so that the door before you will not only open, but be effective. Remember, our adversary is present even when we are right in the midst of what God wants to do in our lives.

Standing Against the Adversary

God has equipped us with the resources we need to stand against our adversaries: the Bible, the Holy Spirit, the powerful name of Jesus Christ, and Jesus' precious blood shed on the cross for us. We need to remember that "the battle is the Lord's" (1 Samuel 17:47) and that God has given us "strength for the battle" and has already overcome our adversaries (2 Samuel 22:40; Psalm 18:39).

Luke 21:15 reiterates this point, "For I will give you words and wisdom that none of your adversaries will be able to resist or contradict." Ephesians 4:27 reminds us to continuously be on guard and never give the devil a foothold in our lives. When we get distracted, we risk the enemy taking control of our lives. We should always be ready to execute God's plans.

Overcoming the Adversary

By obeying the Bible and living in the power of the resurrection of the Lord Jesus Christ and the power of the Holy Spirit, we can get rid of all bitterness, rage, anger, brawling, slander, and malice.

We can be kind and compassionate to one another, forgiving each other quickly, just as in Christ, God forgave us (Ephesians 4:31–32). We have to continue to preach and demonstrate the good news of the gospel. We need to be prepared in season and out of season to correct, rebuke and encourage one another with great patience and careful instruction (2 Timothy 4:2).

Facing Adversity

Let us look at a couple of real-life examples. Despite going blind six weeks after her birth due to the negligence of the physician, Fanny Crosby kept moving forward, kept the faith, and became one of the world's greatest hymn writers. She went on to write 8,000 amazing and meaningful hymns, many of which are still sung today.

Likewise, Horatio Spafford, a prominent American lawyer, penned one of our most moving hymns, *It Is Well With My Soul*, following a family tragedy in which four of his daughters drowned in the middle of the ocean. Both Fanny and Horatio kept their faith even during the horrific calamities they faced.

Exercising Power Against Our Adversary

God distributes to each of us the gifts of the Holy Spirit, and it gives us great joy to see people operating effectively in those gifts. We are also aware that not everyone we pray for receives an answer immediately. Nevertheless, we must persevere in exercising the power that is within us through Jesus Christ. We should not give in to the feeling that we have let down those who eagerly sought prayer from us. We should not feel inadequate if we or a family member or friend has a terminal illness and is not yet healed. We must never underestimate the power of Christ within us. We must resist and overcome the adversary, who always tries to pull down our spirit.

The adversary might parade our guilt every time we want to get closer to God. Take the accusations to the cross of Calvary where Jesus shed His blood for you and me. Take authority in Jesus' name and command Satan to leave. Let us be assured that the prayer of a righteous man produces tremendous results (James 5:16). We are called to be a people of good cheer, for we know our Redeemer lives and He has overcome the world.

The apostle Paul's encouragement is this:

> *"God can bless you abundantly, so that in all things at all times, having all that you need, you will abound in every good work."*
>
> *2 Corinthians 9:8*

May we all find the confidence that comes only from our Lord and Saviour Jesus Christ. We must be bold and courageous in the knowledge that He will never leave us nor forsake us. Jesus Christ is the same yesterday, today, and forever (Hebrews 13:8).

13

A SUPERNATURAL
WAY OF LIFE

People all over the world, of different countries, races and religions have been fascinated by the concept of the supernatural. The Oxford Dictionary defines the word 'supernatural' as *a manifestation or an event considered to be of supernatural origin, attributed to some force beyond scientific understanding or the laws of nature: a supernatural being, unnaturally or extraordinarily great event, or a person.*

As believers, we can explore this concept in a scriptural context. The supernatural refers to understanding God's natural attributes—His character, power, wisdom, and love—from a human perspective. These qualities have been evident from the beginning of creation, with supernatural events unfolding throughout history and continuing today. Understanding the supernatural thus involves recognising the unity of God's attributes at work as a whole.

The following supernatural events reflect the character of our living God and can be seen as a dramatic display of his power:

1. Elijah's sacrifice burned by fire from above when he prayed. The fire of the Lord fell and burned up the sacrifice, the wood, the stones and the soil, and also licked up the water in the trench (1 Kings 18:38).
2. Abraham and Sarah had their promised child in their old age. When Abraham was a hundred years old and Sarah was ninety years old, they had their child of promise; this was a supernatural occurrence. Abraham faced the fact that his body was as good as dead and that Sarah's womb was also dead, without weakening in his faith (Romans 4:19).
3. Jesus raised Lazarus from the dead after four days. On His arrival at the tomb, Jesus called Lazarus in a loud voice, and the dead man walked out. His hands, feet and face were wrapped with grave clothes, indicating that he had indeed died and been buried (John 11:40–45).

God's supernatural intervention in human history always happens when there was a need. God does not orchestrate a supernatural miracle without a purpose or reason that lines up with His Kingdom's purpose. Lazarus was dying, but Jesus delayed his visit to the home of Mary and Martha. He performed the supernatural miracle of bringing Lazarus back to life after he was dead and buried in a tomb for four days. This was to bring glory to His heavenly Father.

When we experience a delay in seeing God's promise being fulfilled in our lives, we can always be sure that His name will be glorified through the delayed fulfillment of His promise. We understand this as a delay, but God never delays. He brings about the fulfillment of His promise perfectly in His time.

Experiencing peace while going through a storm or calamity can be perceived as a supernatural experience. Storms or calamity may come our way, but they will not disturb our inner peace or shake our confidence in God. While all the Egyptians experienced the plagues, the region of Goshen where the Israelites lived was spared.

Most of the time, supernatural events are ignored or taken for granted. We often come across situations that are out of the ordinary. For example, a favour we receive from God and people around us can go unnoticed or taken for granted. A patient's life could be extended beyond the life expectancy predicted medically according to the doctor's report. As we see promises being fulfilled in our day-to-day lives, we need to praise God and share our testimonies with others around us.

Dearly beloved, we need to always be sensitive to the supernatural events happening around us in our homes, communities, cities and nations. We can then praise and thank God for all that He is doing in our midst and our world during our time here on earth. The supernatural way of life will be our way of life if we depend on the Bible and the Holy Spirit, exhibit the fruit of the Holy Spirit, and receive and use the gifts of the Holy Spirit given to us. We can do this by:

1. Meditating on Scripture to strengthen our faith.
2. Relying on the indwelling presence of the Holy Spirit for guidance.
3. Being aware of God's immeasurable love poured out into us, and
4. Living in the hope of our resurrection and eternity.

The love of Christ operates through us with the help of the indwelling Holy Spirit. The fruit of the Holy Spirit expresses Christ to the hurting world around us. We also need God's wisdom to foresee things before they unfold. The gifts of the Holy Spirit are given to us to reach the unreached and be a channel of blessing to those in need. Jesus, when He walked on this earth, performed miracles with the purpose of bringing glory to His heavenly Father. As His 'epistles', we should also point others to our Saviour and Lord Jesus Christ in all that we do.

God's Natural, Our Supernatural

In His love, God sent His Son, Jesus Christ, into this world to die for all. Jesus Christ showed us that faith in Him was required to live a victorious life on this earth. Jesus Christ's resurrection from the dead gives us hope that he will accomplish that for which we have been created. We must love those who hate us and pray for and bless those who curse us. This is not the usual or natural response. We need to remind ourselves that we are salt and light in this hurting world. Therefore, we need to reflect the love of Christ in all situations, which, from our perspective, is a supernatural response.

Expecting the Supernatural

God created the entire universe and continues to have power over all of nature. To save all of humanity, God sent His only Son to die on the cross, demonstrating the power of His love. This is God's love—that He sought us even before we sought Him. His omnipotence was shown in all its splendour when He raised His Son from the dead on the third day. This power of God can be displayed through us His children. We have the Holy Spirit in us to empower us to do the great things that He has in store for us.

Channels of Blessing

We are called to preach the good news to the poor, proclaim freedom to the prisoners, give recovery of sight for the blind, and set the oppressed free in the name of Jesus Christ. In His name, the sick will be healed, the broken-hearted will be comforted, the marginalised will be encouraged and the dead will be raised. To have faith in God is to attune ourselves to the supernatural. To operate in God's love is to go against our natural instincts and follow the prompting of the Holy Spirit. When we are obedient to Him, we become channels of blessing to those in need.

The love of Christ must be our life's foundation. We are called to love the Lord our God with all our heart, soul, strength and mind—and to love our neighbour as ourselves (Luke 10:27). God's wisdom and power will be proven in our lives when we remain in His love.

Our Father in heaven, help us to experience the love of Christ and share His love with all whom we encounter. Let the knowledge of Your Word and wisdom direct us in life. We pray that Your power would be displayed gloriously by the working of Your Holy Spirit in and through us, to bring light into areas of darkness. In Jesus' mighty name, we pray, Amen.

14

WORTHY OF OUR PRAISE

The Lord inhabits the praises of His people, declares Psalm 22:3. This is a promise, and we need to tap into what God has in store for us when we praise Him.

The origin of 'Hallelujah' is 'Praise Jah' (*Jah* is 'God' in Hebrew), as in Psalm 68:4:

> "*Sing to God, sing praises to His name; Extol Him who rides on the clouds, by His name Yah, and rejoice before Him.*"

Praise God, because He is worthy of our praise! In the narration of his vision in the book of Revelation, John encourages us to praise God Almighty, just as the angels and creatures in heaven and on earth praise Him (Revelation 5:11–14).

- Praising God invites the presence of God. In Acts 16:25–26, Paul and Silas were praying and singing hymns to God in prison when suddenly, there was a "violent earthquake" that shook the prison foundations and loosened the prisoners' chains. Praising God enables us to experience His presence, love, power, and wisdom.

- As we praise God, the Lord fights our battles for us. We see this in 2 Chronicles 20:21–22. King Jehoshaphat appointed men to sing praises to the Lord, saying, "Give thanks to the Lord, for his love endures forever." The Lord "set ambushes against the men of Ammon and Moab and Mount Seir who were invading Judah, and they were defeated."

- Praising God is a way of communicating with God and an opportunity to share and testify about God's goodness to people around us. To praise God is to lift His name above all other names. At the name of Jesus, every knee shall bow and every tongue shall confess that He is Lord (Philippians 2:10-11). As we praise and lift His name high, God's glory is seen by all people. The man who was lame from birth was healed through the ministry of Peter and John. People were "filled with wonder and amazement" when they saw the lame man walking and praising God (Acts 3:10).

Jesus' ministry on this earth was only for a little over three years. At that time, the people who followed Him recognised a radical difference in His ministry as they experienced God's supernatural love, power, and wisdom. If we do not praise God for all that He has done in our lives, there will always be someone else who will replace our role. They will praise God for what He has done in their lives—or maybe even the stones or rocks will cry out (Luke 19:37–40)!

Praise as a Weapon

Praise is the ultimate way of communicating with God. It is the highest level of prayer and a sure weapon against the devil. Psalm 8:2 (NIV) declares:

"Through the praise of children and infants you have established a stronghold against your enemies, to silence the foe and the avenger."

Renowned worship leader and songwriter, Darlene Zschech, says:

"Praise is a declaration, a victory cry, proclaiming faith to stand firm in the place God has given you. Praise is a proclamation that the enemy's intent to plunder you will not rock you. Praise declares that you will not be moved by the enemy's attempt to snatch you away."

No wonder we are clearly instructed to praise God!

Psalm 150:6 says:

"Let everything that has breath praise the LORD."

Let us therefore make up our minds to know that our triune God is always on our side, no matter what. He is faithful, good and never changes. His plans are to prosper us and not to harm us (Jeremaih 29:11). His promises are yes and amen in Christ (2 Corinthians 1:20). Let us not forget that every battle we face is the Lord's.

Praise in Every Circumstance

The Scriptures encourage us with these words:

> "Through Jesus, therefore, let us continually offer to God a sacrifice of praise—the fruit of lips that openly profess his name."
>
> *Hebrews 13:15 NIV*

> "Open my lips, Lord, and my mouth will declare your praise. You do not delight in sacrifice, or I would bring it; you do not take pleasure in burnt offerings. My sacrifice, O God, is a broken spirit; a contrite heart you, God, will not despise."
>
> *Psalm 51:15–17 NIV*

When we study the life of King David, we see that although he was given the promise that he would be the future King of Israel, he went through a very difficult time being hunted down relentlessly by King Saul. Yet we read in Psalm 30:11–12 (ESV):

> "You have turned for me my mourning into dancing; you have loosed my sackcloth and clothed me with gladness, that my glory may sing praise to You and not be silent. O Lord my God, I will give thanks to You forever!"

During times of calamity, it is good that people repent and turn to the Lord (2 Chronicles 7:13–14; Hebrews 12:5–11). Nevertheless, we are aware that God does not bring problems our way; it is the enemy who tries to pull our spirits down. The enemy is always a deceiver and a liar. The Bible says that the enemy comes to steal, kill and destroy, but Christ has come to give us life in abundance (John 10:10).

Let us always remember to praise God no matter what the circumstance is, because even if the circumstance seems bad, God is still good. It is easy to praise God when everything around us goes well; it is very difficult to praise God when we see challenges and problems come our way. The God on the mountain is still the God in the valley.

An Acceptable Sacrifice

We praise God because He is worthy. We praise Him to invite His presence into our lives. We praise Him to experience His love, power, and wisdom. We praise God to gain peace and victory, even during troubled times, for He fights our battles. An acceptable sacrifice is the sacrifice of praise with a broken and contrite heart, and with a heart full of joy and gladness for all the goodness that we are experiencing. Let us always be eager to praise our triune God!

15

PRAISE AT ALL TIMES

As God's people, we are made to speak our praise to the Father. In Hebrew, '*halah*' is speaking our praise to the Father, and '*tehillah*' is to sing *halah*. If we express great and extravagant adoration loudly in song, to the point of foolishness in the presence of others, we are giving *tehillah* to the Father. King David said, "I will bless the Lord at all times; His praise shall continually be in my mouth" (Psalm 34:1). He danced and praised God in such a manner in front of his subjects that his wife Michal was not happy about it and ridiculed him.

Praise in the Waiting

We are called to be real in everything we do. We are expected to praise the Lord at all times. When we rejoice in God's goodness in answered prayers, we bring glory to Him. When we continue to serve God while waiting for His answer to our prayer, we bring glory to Him. We will be a source of encouragement to believers and non-believers alike when we display God's peace and happiness amidst our despairing situation. Our life story will then bring those who are hurting to focus on Jesus Christ.

When Paul and Silas were in prison, they sang praises to God (Acts 16:24-26). Joseph, while waiting for his dream to come true, endured the wrongdoings of his brothers, the pit and the prison before he was made prime minister of Egypt. David, waiting to be seated on the throne according to God's promise, was hunted day and night by King Saul. Even when he had the opportunity to kill King Saul, David did not touch the Lord's anointed. Abraham and Sarah waited for their promised child, believing in the supernatural, because both had passed the age of childbearing. The faith and hope these men and women had in the promise-keeping God is exceptional and highly commendable.

Those of us who are waiting on God to see His promises fulfilled in our lives can ask ourselves, "Are we limiting our knowledge and understanding of Almighty God to a mere miracle?" Let us understand that nothing is difficult for Him. As it says in Jeremiah 32:27 (NIV), "I am the Lord, the God of all mankind. Is anything too hard for me?" Let us continue to believe in Almighty God, the maker of heaven and earth. He is the God who sent His only begotten Son to this world to die on our behalf. This plan was laid long before the foundation of the world. That is how much He loves us. Will He not do whatever we ask in the name of His Son Jesus?

Glory to His Name

Do our neighbours, friends or colleagues give thanks to God for our lives of witness that bring glory to God's name? Are we able to say with the apostle Paul that we know what it is to be in want and what it is to have plenty? Can we stretch this to another level and say that we are thankful to God for who He is to us rather than what He can do for us?

Miracles do happen, and they bring glory to His name. When Joseph was put in the pit, the prison and then taken to the palace, he did not let go of the dream and vision that he had. He gave glory to God whenever he had an opportunity, even when he stood before Pharaoh. Let us always remember that our God is seated on His throne, and He reigns forever. Whatever our current circumstance may be, let us be strong and of good courage, for He is always there to fight the battle that belongs to Him.

Andy Stanley, in his book *Deep and Wide*, commends the faith he sees in people whose prayers are unanswered:

> "As our team continued to wrestle with the relationship of faith and spiritual maturity, we all agreed that we were way more inspired by the people who have the kind of faith that endures a no from God than those who claim their faith arm twisted a yes out of Him. Big faith is a sign of big maturity".[2]

In 1 Peter 1:1–12, we read that even angels are eager to watch the fulfilment of the glories that would follow when Jesus Christ is revealed. When we are asking God to answer a question or solve a problem, or while we are eagerly waiting for His promise to be fulfilled, we need to continue to serve Him diligently. The apostle Paul says in 2 Corinthians 4:8–9, we are "hard-pressed on every side, yet not crushed; we are

---

2   Andy Stanley, *Deep and Wide: Creating Churches Unchurched People Love to Attend*, 2012 North Point Ministries, Atlanta, USA.

perplexed, but not in despair; persecuted, but not forsaken; struck down, but not destroyed." We are comforted by our Lord and Saviour Jesus Christ in our suffering, which enables us to comfort others (2 Corinthians 1:3–4).

We love God for who He is and not for what He will do. Can we say with Paul that God loves us even when we are going through times of testing and tribulation? After all,

> *"Who shall separate us from the love of Christ? Shall trouble or hardship or persecution or famine or nakedness or danger or sword?"*
> *Romans 8:35 NIV*

When we continue to praise God in all situations, it is like a bulwark or fortification against despair. The Lord is faithful to those who love Him and keep His commandments.

> *"Therefore know that the Lord your God, He is God, the faithful God who keeps covenant and mercy for a thousand generations with those who love Him and keep His commandments . . ."*
> *Deuteronomy 7:9*

> *". . . the Lord is faithful, who will establish you and guard you from the evil one."*
> *2 Thessalonians 3:3*

Let us remember that we are sojourners on planet Earth, and though we have not seen Him, we love Him; and even though we do not see Him now, we believe in Him and are filled with inexpressible and glorious joy, for we are receiving the end result of our faith, the salvation of our souls (1 Peter 1:8–9).

May the God of peace and all comfort continue to sustain us and keep us.

"Now to him who is able to do immeasurably more than all we ask or imagine, according to his power that is at work within us, to him be glory in the church and in Christ Jesus throughout all generations, for ever and ever! Amen."

Ephesians 3:20–21 NIV

16

ALL THINGS
MADE NEW

"He who was seated on the throne said, 'I am making everything new!' Then he said, "Write this down, for these words are trustworthy and true."

Revelation 21:5 NIV

When we are in the valley, the Lord turns our situation around for us. In Jeremiah's laments, he mentions that God's mercy and compassions are new every morning. He also declares unto the Lord, "Great is Your faithfulness" (Lamentations 3:23). Our only hope is in our Lord; He is our inheritance. God makes everything new. He even blesses us with an abundance of grain and new wine (Genesis 27:28; Deuteronomy 7:13).

We see again in Revelation 21:5–7 that God Almighty makes everything new. In this passage, the New Jerusalem comes down as a bride, the Lord makes a new heaven and a new earth, and the old heaven and the old earth pass away.

However, even today, God is making all things new. He is doing everything afresh. His mercies are new every morning. He is the source of the living water of life (John 4:14) and He enables us to inherit all His blessings when we are victorious in all our trials and battles (Matthew 5:5). This is what he has done since the creation of the universe, and it is what He will always do:

1. **New thing:** "For I am about to do something new. See, I have already begun! Do you not see it? I will make a pathway through the wilderness. I will create rivers in the dry wasteland." (Isaiah 43:19 NLT)

2. **New person:** "This means that anyone who belongs to Christ has become a new person. The old life is gone; a new life has begun!" (2 Corinthians 5:17 NLT)

3. **New strength:** "But those who trust in the Lord will find new strength. They will soar high on wings like eagles. They will run and not grow weary. They will walk and not faint." (Isaiah 40:31 NLT)

4. **New thoughts:** "Don't copy the behaviour and customs of this world, but let God transform you into a new person by changing the way you think. Then you will learn to know God's will for you, which is good and pleasing and perfect." (Romans 12:2 NLT)

5. **New heart:** "And I will give you a new heart, and I will put a new spirit in you. I will take out your stony, stubborn heart and give you a tender, responsive heart." (Ezekiel 36:26 NLT)

6. **New spirit:** "Create in me a clean heart, O God. Renew a loyal spirit within me." (Psalm 51:10 NLT)

7. **New birth:** "Praise be to the God and Father of our Lord Jesus Christ! In his great mercy he has given us new birth into a living hope through the resurrection of Jesus Christ from the dead . . ." (1 Peter 1:3 NIV)

8. **New commandment:** "A new command I give you: Love
   one another. As I have loved you, so you must love one
   another." (John 13:34 NIV)

Friends, when we are born again, old things pass away and
behold, *all things* are made new! Jesus has entered into a
entirely new covenant with us—a covenant of the Spirit.

> *"He has made us competent as ministers of a new
> covenant—not of the letter but of the Spirit; for the letter
> kills, but the Spirit gives life."*
> 2 Corinthians 3:6 NIV

This covenant is of righteousness and not condemnation,
enabling us to see the glory that lasts and does not fade. We
are now able to have direct access to God. There is no veil
between us and Him. Our calling is to show the love of Christ
that is in us to others and to do His will. Jesus reaffirms His
will for us in the Gospel of John,

> *"Very truly I tell you, whoever believes in me will do the
> works I have been doing, and they will do even greater
> things than these, because I am going to the Father . . .
> Whoever has My commands and keeps them is the one
> who loves Me. The one who loves Me will be loved by My
> Father, and I too will love them and show myself to them."*
> John 14:12, 21 NIV

Christ's mission is lucidly presented in Isaiah 61:1–3 and
reiterated in Luke 4:18.

> *"The Spirit of the Sovereign Lord is on me, because the
> Lord has anointed me to proclaim good news to the poor.
> He has sent me to bind up the brokenhearted, to proclaim
> freedom for the captives and release from darkness for the*

prisoners, to proclaim the year of the Lord's favour and the day of vengeance of our God, to comfort all who mourn, and provide for those who grieve in Zion—to bestow on them a crown of beauty instead of ashes, the oil of joy instead of mourning, and a garment of praise instead of a spirit of despair. They will be called oaks of righteousness, a planting of the Lord for the display of His splendor."

Isaiah 61:1–3 NIV

As Christ's epistles, we are to walk in our Lord and Saviour Jesus Christ's footsteps, bringing wholeness to the people around us—healing of spirit, soul, and body. We may be surprised by a turn in our life or a situation that arises, but we know that all things are filtered by our Father's loving fingers, whether big or small. Troubles may come on account of our own mistakes or as an attack from the enemy as we desire to grow in spiritual intimacy with our God. Whatever the reason, difficulties are sure to lead us into a new season. Therefore, we will not fear, for our God makes everything new.

Let us face change with the Father's perspective. Let us see with eyes of faith that He has started to make everything new. When we believe in the Lord, we will see the Red Sea part. We will praise and worship Him as we walk through any situation, for we know our Redeemer lives. One day, we will hear Him say,

"Well done, my good and faithful servant."

Matthew 25:21 NLT

Praise be to His name forever!

May the love of our heavenly Father, the fellowship of His Son Jesus Christ, and the sweet presence of the Holy Spirit rest and abide with us now and always. Amen.

ACKNOWLEDGEMENTS

With love and thanks to my wife Harshala for her enduring encouragement in writing this book.

A sincere note of gratitude to our pastors, church leaders, connect group friends and family for their contribution to my faith life and their unwavering belief and support.

I am truly thankful for the patience and expertise of Anya and Jeff McKee of Wild Side Publishing for their invaluable assistance in editing this book.

ABOUT THE AUTHOR

Peter Emmanuel, originally from Chennai, India, has resided in Auckland, New Zealand, for over 24 years with his wife, Harshala. He holds a degree in electronics and instrumentation engineering and a master's degree in business management and has been in the corporate business for over 35 years with various multinational corporations.

Peter and Harshala actively collaborate with local churches and Christian organizations in New Zealand, India, Australia, and other nations. They have pursued theological studies through Haggai International and Veritas College International (Perth) and are marriage mentors with FamilyLife NZ.

With over two decades of involvement in Christian ministry, Peter is a devoted follower of Jesus Christ. His ministry focuses on mentoring men, operating in the power of the Holy Spirit, and teaching the Word of God in men's groups, connect groups, and churches. He is deeply committed to guiding men and families toward a closer relationship with God, equipping them to build strong, fulfilling marriages, and fostering a positive impact within their communities.

JESU BERACAH

MINISTRIES

Peter and Harshala Emmanuel, the founders of *Jesu Beracah Ministries*, embarked on a faith-led journey from their homeland of India to New Zealand, the 'Land of the Long White Cloud,' in 2001.

Their mission is to serve the community by ministering and introducing individuals to Jesus Christ. They are dedicated to discipling individuals and couples, encouraging total reliance on God's Word and guidance through the Holy Spirit.

Actively partnering with local churches and Christian organizations in New Zealand, India and beyond, they engage in teaching and preaching the Word of God, mentoring young people, counselling individuals and families, and ministering through the gifts of the Holy Spirit. As members of Elim Christian Centre, Botany, they lead a Bible study every Thursday. Their messages are accessible via their website and Zion FM Web Radio.

Firmly rooted in faith in the Heavenly Father, the Son—Lord Jesus Christ—and the Holy Spirit, their vision, as inspired by Hebrews 12:1-2, is to live humbly in service to Christ and to fulfill the calling to be 'fishers of men'.

For more information, please visit **www.jesuberacah.com** or email **harshala@jesuberacah.com**